MW01198865

HOW TO BE A FEMINIST (FOR LITTLE GIRLS & BOYS) © 2019 by Maxine Russell

Brown Paper Press

6475 E. Pacific Coast Highway, #329
Long Beach, CA 90803

Library of Congress Control Number: 2019942768

ISBN: 978-1-941932-15-5

14 13 12 11 10 / 10 9 8 7 6 5 4 3 2 1

HOW TO BE A FEMINIST
(FOR LITTLE GIRLS & BOYS)

Written & Illustrated by
Maxine Russell

Maxine

♡

BROWN PAPER PRESS
LONG BEACH, CA

What is a feminist?

A feminist is a person who
believes that men and
women should be treated the
same way.

Pretty SIMPLE, right?

Well here's where it gets a
little confusing.

Some people believe that men and women should not be equal. Some people believe that men should have more power than women.

And since there are those kinds of
people in the world, we have
FEMINISTS.

They are a little like superheroes.
They make the world a better place by
doing their part to make the world
fair for everyone.

And ANYONE can be a feminist!

Boys, girls, moms, dads, aunts, uncles, grandparents, anyone!

But how?

Being a feminist is EASY.

Feminists speak up for what they believe, and they speak up for girls.

Being a feminist is being
PROUD of being a feminist.

And not being afraid
to tell people that.

Being a feminist is paying close ATTENTION to when a girl is being treated differently than a boy.

Like, if a boy says a girl can't have
a toy because she is a girl.

Being a feminist is making sure
that women have just as many
RIGHTS as men do.

Being a feminist can mean
that you feel alone sometimes.

Like nobody is on your side.

But when you feel that way, just know
that a CROWD OF FEMINISTS
has your back.

And those feminists will fight for you,
just as much as you fight for them.

Maxine Russell is a thirteen-year-old middle school student, aspiring filmmaker, and feminist. She lives with her parents in Long Beach, California.

BROWN
PAPER
PRESS

Brown Paper Press engages readers
on topics of contemporary culture
through quality writing and thoughtful
design. Unbound by genre, our press
delivers socially relevant works that
advise, guide, inspire, and amuse.
We champion authors with new
perspectives, strong voices, and
original ideas that might just change
the world.

For more information, visit
brownpaperpress.com or follow us
on Instagram, Twitter or Facebook @
BrownPaperPress.

CPSIA information can be obtained
at www.ICGtesting.com
Printed in the USA
BVHW022138260120
570579BV00001B/1